_____

_____

_____

_____

Praise God in His sanctuary; praise Him in His mighty heavens. Praise Him
for His acts of power; praise Him for His surpassing greatness.

Psalm 150:1-2

_____

"I know the plans I have for you," declares the Lord, "plans to prosper you and not to harm you, plans to give you hope and a future."

Jeremiah 29:11

I will bless You as long as I live; in Your name I will lift up my hands.
Psalm 63:4

_____

"Come to Me, all of you who are weary and carry
heavy burdens, and I will give you rest."
Matthew 11:28

May the Lord of peace Himself give you peace at all times and in every way.
2 Thessalonians 3:16

_____

Create in me a clean heart, O God, and renew a steadfast spirit within me.
Psalm 51:10

_____

_____

_____

_____

_____

_____

_____

_____

_____

_____

_____

_____

_____

_____

_____

_____

_____

_____

_____

_____

_____

Sing for joy, O heavens, and exult, O earth; break forth,
O mountains, into singing! For the LORD has comforted His people.
Isaiah 49:13

_____

"Anything is possible if a person believes."
Mark 9:23

"Peace I leave with you; My peace I give to you...
Let not your hearts be troubled, neither let them be afraid."
John 14:27

_____

Give thanks to the God of gods ... Give thanks to the Lord of lords ...
Give thanks to the God of heaven, for His steadfast love endures forever.
Psalm 136:2-3, 26

"No eye has seen, no ear has heard, and no mind has imagined
what God has prepared for those who love Him."
1 Corinthians 2:9

_____

Let us hold unswervingly to the hope we profess,
for He who promised is faithful.
Hebrews 10:23

Draw near to God, and He will draw near to you.
James 4:8

_____

Praise the name of the Lord, for His name alone is exalted;
His majesty is above earth and heaven.

Psalm 148:13

_____

_____

_____

_____

_____

_____

_____

_____

_____

_____

_____

_____

_____

_____

_____

_____

_____

_____

_____

_____

_____

_____

"I am with you always, even to the end of the age."
Matthew 28:20

The Lord is good to all; He has compassion on all He has made.
Psalm 145:9

_____

_____

_____

_____

_____

_____

_____

_____

_____

_____

_____

_____

_____

_____

_____

_____

_____

_____

_____

_____

_____

_____

_____

_____

He who has begun a good work in you will complete it
until the day of Jesus Christ.
Philippians 1:6

_____

_____

_____

_____

_____

_____

_____

_____

_____

_____

_____

_____

_____

_____

_____

_____

_____

_____

_____

_____

_____

_____

_____

_____

_____

"Whoever comes to Me I will never cast out... For this is the will of My Father, that everyone who looks on the Son and believes in Him should have eternal life."

John 6:37, 40

Thank You for making me so wonderfully complex!
Your workmanship is marvelous—how well I know it.
Psalm 139:14

If anything is excellent or praiseworthy—think about such things.
Philippians 4:8

_____

_____

_____

_____

_____

_____

_____

_____

_____

_____

_____

_____

_____

_____

_____

_____

_____

_____

_____

_____

_____

_____

Trust in the LORD forever,
for the LORD, the LORD Himself, is the Rock eternal.
Isaiah 26:4

"You are the Lord, You alone. You have made heaven, the heaven of heavens ...
the earth and all that is on it ... and You preserve all of them."

Nehemiah 9:6

We know that God causes everything to work together for the good of those
who love God and are called according to His purpose for them.

Romans 8:28

God has said, "Never will I leave you; never will I forsake you."
So we say with confidence, "The Lord is my helper; I will not be afraid."
Hebrews 13:5-6

Happy are those who hear the joyful call to worship, for they will walk in the light of Your presence, LORD.... They exult in Your righteousness.

Psalm 89:15-16

_____

God is able to make all grace abound to you, so that having all sufficiency
in all things at all times, you may abound in every good work.
2 Corinthians 9:8

Sing a new song to the Lord! Sing His praises from the ends of the earth!

Isaiah 42:10

The Lord is good, a refuge in times of trouble. He cares for those who trust in Him.
Nahum 1:7

Cast all your anxiety on Him because He cares for you.
1 Peter 5:7

_____

"Blessing and glory and wisdom and thanksgiving and honor and
power and might be to our God forever and ever! Amen."
Revelation 7:12

_____

"May the LORD bless you and protect you. May the LORD smile on you and be gracious to you. May the LORD show you His favor and give you His peace."

Numbers 6:24-26

_____

_____

_____

_____

_____

_____

_____

_____

_____

_____

_____

_____

_____

_____

_____

_____

_____

_____

_____

_____

_____

_____

"The Lord your God is with you, He is mighty to save. He will take great delight in you,
He will quiet you with His love, He will rejoice over you with singing."
Zephaniah 3:17

_____

_____

_____

_____

_____

_____

_____

_____

_____

_____

_____

_____

_____

_____

_____

_____

_____

_____

_____

_____

_____

I will instruct you and teach you in the way you should go;
I will guide you with My eye.
Psalm 32:8

_____

For You are my rock and my fortress; and for Your
name's sake You lead me and guide me.
Psalm 31:3

_____

_____

_____

_____

_____

_____

_____

_____

_____

_____

_____

_____

_____

_____

_____

_____

_____

_____

_____

_____

_____

_____

_____

Search me, O God, and know my heart; test me and know my anxious thoughts.
Psalm 139:23

_____

"I am the living bread that came down from heaven.
If anyone eats of this bread, he will live forever."
John 6:51

Those who wait on the Lord shall renew their strength;
they shall mount up with wings like eagles.
Isaiah 40:31

_____

"I came that they may have life and have it abundantly."
John 10:10

O Lᴏʀᴅ, I will honor and praise Your name, for You are my God.
You do such wonderful things!

Isaiah 25:1

With You is the fountain of life; in Your light do we see light.
Psalm 36:9

_____

_____

_____

_____

_____

_____

_____

_____

_____

_____

_____

_____

_____

_____

_____

_____

_____

_____

_____

_____

_____

For as members of one body you are called to live in peace.
And always be thankful.
Colossians 3:15

_____

Pour out your hearts to Him, for God is our refuge.
Psalm 62:8

Be kind to one another, tenderhearted, forgiving one another,
even as God in Christ forgave you.
Ephesians 4:32

_____

Let not steadfast love and faithfulness forsake you ... write them on the tablet of your heart. So you will find favor and good success in the sight of God and man.

Proverbs 3:3-4

Day by day the LORD takes care of the innocent,
and they will receive an inheritance that lasts forever.
Psalm 37:18

_____

Strive for full restoration, encourage one another, be of one mind,
live in peace. And the God of love and peace will be with you.
2 Corinthians 13:11

Godliness with contentment is great gain.
1 Timothy 6:6

May He give you the desire of your heart and
make all your plans succeed.
Psalm 20:4

_____

Every good gift and every perfect gift is from above.
James 1:17

_____

_____

_____

_____

_____

_____

_____

_____

_____

_____

_____

_____

_____

_____

_____

_____

_____

_____

_____

_____

May the God of peace ... equip you with everything good for doing His will ...
through Jesus Christ, to whom be glory for ever and ever.
Hebrews 13:20-21

How precious to me are Your thoughts, O God! How vast is the sum of them!

_____

As the deer longs for streams of water, so I long for You,
O God. I thirst for God, the living God.
Psalm 42:1-2

_____

_____

_____

_____

_____

_____

_____

_____

_____

_____

_____

_____

_____

_____

_____

_____

_____

_____

_____

_____

_____

_____

_____

_____

_____

"I will not forget you! See, I have engraved you on the palms of My hands."
Isaiah 49:15-16

_____

Know that the LORD, He is God! It is He who made us, and we
are His; we are His people, and the sheep of His pasture.
Psalm 100:3

"If you abide in Me, and My words abide in you, you will ask
what you desire, and it shall be done for you."
John 15:7

_____

Lead me in Your truth and teach me, for You are the God
of my salvation; for You I wait all the day long.
Psalm 25:5

_____

_____

_____

_____

_____

_____

_____

_____

_____

_____

_____

_____

_____

_____

_____

_____

_____

_____

_____

_____

_____

_____

_____

_____

_____

"Give, and you will receive. Your gift will return to you in full—pressed down, shaken together to make room for more, running over."

Luke 6:38

_____

He will keep you strong to the end so that you will be free
from all blame on the day when our Lord Jesus Christ returns.
1 Corinthians 1:8

The reward for trusting Him will be the salvation of your souls.
1 Peter 1:9

_____

He who earnestly seeks good finds favor.
Proverbs 11:27

My soul clings to You; Your right hand upholds me.
Psalm 63:8

May the God of hope fill you with all joy and peace as you trust in Him,
so that you may overflow with hope by the power of the Holy Spirit.
Romans 15:13

_____

_____

_____

_____

_____

_____

_____

_____

_____

_____

_____

_____

_____

_____

_____

_____

_____

_____

_____

_____

_____

Keep me as the apple of Your eye; hide me in the shadow of Your wings.
Psalm 17:8

_____

Because of the Lord's great love we are not consumed,
for His compassions never fail.
Lamentations 3:22

_____

_____
_____
_____
_____
_____
_____
_____
_____
_____
_____
_____
_____
_____
_____
_____
_____
_____
_____
_____
_____
_____
_____
_____
_____

Praise God in His sanctuary; praise Him in His mighty heavens. Praise Him
for His acts of power; praise Him for His surpassing greatness.
Psalm 150:1-2

"I know the plans I have for you," declares the Lord, "plans to prosper you and not to harm you, plans to give you hope and a future."

Jeremiah 29:11

I will bless You as long as I live; in Your name I will lift up my hands.
Psalm 63:4

_____

"Come to Me, all of you who are weary and carry
heavy burdens, and I will give you rest."
Matthew 11:28

May the Lord of peace Himself give you peace at all times and in every way.
2 Thessalonians 3:16

_____

Create in me a clean heart, O God, and renew a steadfast spirit within me.
Psalm 51:10

Sing for joy, O heavens, and exult, O earth; break forth,
O mountains, into singing! For the LORD has comforted His people.
Isaiah 49:13

_____

"Anything is possible if a person believes."
Mark 9:23

"Peace I leave with you; My peace I give to you...
Let not your hearts be troubled, neither let them be afraid."

John 14:27

Give thanks to the God of gods ... Give thanks to the Lord of lords ...
Give thanks to the God of heaven, for His steadfast love endures forever.
Psalm 136:2-3, 26

_____

_____

_____

_____

_____

_____

_____

_____

_____

_____

_____

_____

_____

_____

_____

_____

_____

_____

_____

_____

_____

_____

"No eye has seen, no ear has heard, and no mind has imagined
what God has prepared for those who love Him."
1 Corinthians 2:9

_____

Let us hold unswervingly to the hope we profess,
for He who promised is faithful.
Hebrews 10:23

_____

_____
_____
_____
_____
_____
_____
_____
_____
_____
_____
_____
_____
_____
_____
_____
_____
_____
_____
_____
_____
_____

Draw near to God, and He will draw near to you.
James 4:8

Praise the name of the LORD, for His name alone is exalted;
His majesty is above earth and heaven.
Psalm 148:13

The Lord is good to all; He has compassion on all He has made.
Psalm 145:9

He who has begun a good work in you will complete it
until the day of Jesus Christ.
Philippians 1:6

"Whoever comes to Me I will never cast out... For this is the will of My Father, that everyone who looks on the Son and believes in Him should have eternal life."
John 6:37, 40

_____

_____

_____

_____

_____

_____

_____

_____

_____

_____

_____

_____

_____

_____

_____

_____

_____

_____

_____

_____

Thank You for making me so wonderfully complex!
Your workmanship is marvelous—how well I know it.
Psalm 139:14

If anything is excellent or praiseworthy—think about such things.
Philippians 4:8

Trust in the LORD forever,
for the LORD, the LORD Himself, is the Rock eternal.
Isaiah 26:4

_____

We know that God causes everything to work together for the good of those
who love God and are called according to His purpose for them.
Romans 8:28

_____

God has said, "Never will I leave you; never will I forsake you."
So we say with confidence, "The Lord is my helper; I will not be afraid."
Hebrews 13:5-6

Happy are those who hear the joyful call to worship, for they will walk in
the light of Your presence, Lord.... They exult in Your righteousness.

Psalm 89:15-16

_____

God is able to make all grace abound to you, so that having all sufficiency
in all things at all times, you may abound in every good work.
2 Corinthians 9:8

Sing a new song to the LORD! Sing His praises from the ends of the earth!
Isaiah 42:10

The Lord is good, a refuge in times of trouble. He cares for those who trust in Him.
Nahum 1:7

Cast all your anxiety on Him because He cares for you.
1 Peter 5:7

"Blessing and glory and wisdom and thanksgiving and honor and
power and might be to our God forever and ever! Amen."
Revelation 7:12

"May the LORD bless you and protect you. May the LORD smile on you and be gracious to you. May the LORD show you His favor and give you His peace."

Numbers 6:24-26

"The LORD your God is with you, He is mighty to save. He will take great delight in you, He will quiet you with His love, He will rejoice over you with singing."

Zephaniah 3:17

I will instruct you and teach you in the way you should go;
I will guide you with My eye.

Psalm 32:8

For You are my rock and my fortress; and for Your
name's sake You lead me and guide me.
Psalm 31:3

Search me, O God, and know my heart; test me and know my anxious thoughts.
Psalm 139:23

_____

"I am the living bread that came down from heaven.
If anyone eats of this bread, he will live forever."
John 6:51

Those who wait on the LORD shall renew their strength;
they shall mount up with wings like eagles.

Isaiah 40:31

_____
_____
_____
_____
_____
_____
_____
_____
_____
_____
_____
_____
_____
_____
_____
_____
_____
_____
_____
_____
_____

"I came that they may have life and have it abundantly."
John 10:10

O Lord, I will honor and praise Your name, for You are my God.
You do such wonderful things!
Isaiah 25:1

With You is the fountain of life; in Your light do we see light.
Psalm 36:9

For as members of one body you are called to live in peace.
And always be thankful.
Colossians 3:15

Pour out your hearts to Him, for God is our refuge.
Psalm 62:8

Be kind to one another, tenderhearted, forgiving one another,
even as God in Christ forgave you.
Ephesians 4:32

Let not steadfast love and faithfulness forsake you ... write them on the tablet of your heart. So you will find favor and good success in the sight of God and man.

Proverbs 3:3-4

Day by day the LORD takes care of the innocent,
and they will receive an inheritance that lasts forever.
Psalm 37:18

Strive for full restoration, encourage one another, be of one mind,
live in peace. And the God of love and peace will be with you.
2 Corinthians 13:11

_____

Godliness with contentment is great gain.
1 Timothy 6:6

May He give you the desire of your heart and
make all your plans succeed.
Psalm 20:4

Every good gift and every perfect gift is from above.
James 1:17

_____

May the God of peace ... equip you with everything good for doing His will ...
through Jesus Christ, to whom be glory for ever and ever.
Hebrews 13:20-21

How precious to me are Your thoughts, O God! How vast is the sum of them!
Psalm 139:17

_____

As the deer longs for streams of water, so I long for You,
O God. I thirst for God, the living God.
Psalm 42:1-2

"I will not forget you! See, I have engraved you on the palms of My hands."
Isaiah 49:15-16

_____

Know that the LORD, He is God! It is He who made us, and we
are His; we are His people, and the sheep of His pasture.
Psalm 100:3

_____

_____

_____

_____

_____

_____

_____

_____

_____

_____

_____

_____

_____

_____

_____

_____

_____

_____

_____

_____

_____

_____

_____

_____

"If you abide in Me, and My words abide in you, you will ask
what you desire, and it shall be done for you."
John 15:7

Lead me in Your truth and teach me, for You are the God
of my salvation; for You I wait all the day long.
Psalm 25:5

"Give, and you will receive. Your gift will return to you in full—pressed down, shaken together to make room for more, running over."
Luke 6:38

_____

He will keep you strong to the end so that you will be free
from all blame on the day when our Lord Jesus Christ returns.
1 Corinthians 1:8

_____

The reward for trusting Him will be the salvation of your souls.
1 Peter 1:9

_____

He who earnestly seeks good finds favor.
Proverbs 11:27

My soul clings to You; Your right hand upholds me.
Psalm 63:8

_____

May the God of hope fill you with all joy and peace as you trust in Him,
so that you may overflow with hope by the power of the Holy Spirit.
Romans 15:13

Keep me as the apple of Your eye; hide me in the shadow of Your wings.
Psalm 17:8

_____

Because of the Lord's great love we are not consumed,
for His compassions never fail.
Lamentations 3:22

Praise God in His sanctuary; praise Him in His mighty heavens. Praise Him for His acts of power; praise Him for His surpassing greatness.

Psalm 150:1-2

"I know the plans I have for you," declares the Lord, "plans to prosper you and not to harm you, plans to give you hope and a future."
Jeremiah 29:11

I will bless You as long as I live; in Your name I will lift up my hands.

Psalm 63:4

_____

"Come to Me, all of you who are weary and carry
heavy burdens, and I will give you rest."
Matthew 11:28

_____

_____

_____

_____

_____

_____

_____

_____

_____

_____

_____

_____

_____

_____

_____

_____

_____

_____

_____

_____

_____

May the Lord of peace Himself give you peace at all times and in every way.
2 Thessalonians 3:16

_____

Create in me a clean heart, O God, and renew a steadfast spirit within me.
Psalm 51:10

Sing for joy, O heavens, and exult, O earth; break forth,
O mountains, into singing! For the LORD has comforted His people.

Isaiah 49:13

_____

"Anything is possible if a person believes."
Mark 9:23

_____

_____
_____
_____
_____
_____
_____
_____
_____
_____
_____
_____
_____
_____
_____
_____
_____
_____
_____
_____
_____
_____
_____
_____
_____

"Peace I leave with you; My peace I give to you...
Let not your hearts be troubled, neither let them be afraid."
John 14:27

_____

Give thanks to the God of gods ... Give thanks to the Lord of lords ...
Give thanks to the God of heaven, for His steadfast love endures forever.
Psalm 136:2-3, 26

_____

_____
_____
_____
_____
_____
_____
_____
_____
_____
_____
_____
_____
_____
_____
_____
_____
_____
_____
_____
_____
_____
_____
_____

"No eye has seen, no ear has heard, and no mind has imagined
what God has prepared for those who love Him."
1 Corinthians 2:9

_____

Let us hold unswervingly to the hope we profess,
for He who promised is faithful.
Hebrews 10:23

Draw near to God, and He will draw near to you.
James 4:8

_____

Praise the name of the LORD, for His name alone is exalted;
His majesty is above earth and heaven.
Psalm 148:13

_____

_____

_____

_____

_____

_____

_____

_____

_____

_____

_____

_____

_____

_____

_____

_____

_____

_____

_____

_____

_____

_____

"I am with you always, even to the end of the age."
Matthew 28:20

_____

The LORD is good to all; He has compassion on all He has made.
Psalm 145:9

_____

_____

_____

_____

_____

_____

_____

_____

_____

_____

_____

_____

_____

_____

_____

_____

_____

_____

_____

_____

_____

He who has begun a good work in you will complete it
until the day of Jesus Christ.
Philippians 1:6

_____

_____

_____

_____

_____

_____

_____

_____

_____

_____

_____

_____

_____

_____

_____

_____

_____

_____

_____

_____

_____

_____

_____

"Whoever comes to Me I will never cast out... For this is the will of My Father, that everyone who looks on the Son and believes in Him should have eternal life."

John 6:37, 40

Thank You for making me so wonderfully complex!
Your workmanship is marvelous—how well I know it.

Psalm 139:14

_____

If anything is excellent or praiseworthy—think about such things.
Philippians 4:8

Trust in the LORD forever,
for the LORD, the LORD Himself, is the Rock eternal.
Isaiah 26:4

_____

"You are the LORD, You alone. You have made heaven, the heaven of heavens ...
the earth and all that is on it ... and You preserve all of them."
Nehemiah 9:6

We know that God causes everything to work together for the good of those
who love God and are called according to His purpose for them.

Romans 8:28

God has said, "Never will I leave you; never will I forsake you."
So we say with confidence, "The Lord is my helper; I will not be afraid."
Hebrews 13:5-6

Happy are those who hear the joyful call to worship, for they will walk in
the light of Your presence, Lᴏʀᴅ.... They exult in Your righteousness.

Psalm 89:15-16

_____

God is able to make all grace abound to you, so that having all sufficiency
in all things at all times, you may abound in every good work.
2 Corinthians 9:8

Sing a new song to the Lord! Sing His praises from the ends of the earth!
Isaiah 42:10

_____

The LORD is good, a refuge in times of trouble. He cares for those who trust in Him.
Nahum 1:7

Cast all your anxiety on Him because He cares for you.
1 Peter 5:7

_____

"Blessing and glory and wisdom and thanksgiving and honor and
power and might be to our God forever and ever! Amen."
Revelation 7:12

"May the Lord bless you and protect you. May the Lord smile on you and be gracious to you. May the Lord show you His favor and give you His peace."
Numbers 6:24-26

"The LORD your God is with you, He is mighty to save. He will take great delight in you, He will quiet you with His love, He will rejoice over you with singing."
Zephaniah 3:17

I will instruct you and teach you in the way you should go;
I will guide you with My eye.
Psalm 32:8

For You are my rock and my fortress; and for Your
name's sake You lead me and guide me.
Psalm 31:3

Search me, O God, and know my heart; test me and know my anxious thoughts.
Psalm 139:23

_____

"I am the living bread that came down from heaven.
If anyone eats of this bread, he will live forever."
John 6:51

Those who wait on the LORD shall renew their strength;
they shall mount up with wings like eagles.
Isaiah 40:31

_____

"I came that they may have life and have it abundantly."
John 10:10

O Lᴏʀᴅ, I will honor and praise Your name, for You are my God.
You do such wonderful things!

Isaiah 25:1

With You is the fountain of life; in Your light do we see light.

Psalm 36:9

For as members of one body you are called to live in peace.
And always be thankful.

Colossians 3:15

_____

Pour out your hearts to Him, for God is our refuge.
Psalm 62:8

Be kind to one another, tenderhearted, forgiving one another,
even as God in Christ forgave you.
Ephesians 4:32

_____

Let not steadfast love and faithfulness forsake you ... write them on the tablet of
your heart. So you will find favor and good success in the sight of God and man.
Proverbs 3:3-4

Day by day the LORD takes care of the innocent,
and they will receive an inheritance that lasts forever.
Psalm 37:18

_____

Strive for full restoration, encourage one another, be of one mind,
live in peace. And the God of love and peace will be with you.
2 Corinthians 13:11

Godliness with contentment is great gain.
1 Timothy 6:6

_____

May He give you the desire of your heart and
make all your plans succeed.
Psalm 20:4

_____

_____
_____
_____
_____
_____
_____
_____
_____
_____
_____
_____
_____
_____
_____
_____
_____
_____
_____
_____
_____
_____
_____
_____

Every good gift and every perfect gift is from above.
James 1:17

_____

May the God of peace ... equip you with everything good for doing His will ...
through Jesus Christ, to whom be glory for ever and ever.
Hebrews 13:20-21

How precious to me are Your thoughts, O God! How vast is the sum of them!
Psalm 139:17

_____

As the deer longs for streams of water, so I long for You,
O God. I thirst for God, the living God.
Psalm 42:1-2

"I will not forget you! See, I have engraved you on the palms of My hands."
Isaiah 49:15-16

_____

Know that the LORD, He is God! It is He who made us, and we
are His; we are His people, and the sheep of His pasture.

Psalm 100:3

_____

_____

_____

_____

_____

_____

_____

_____

_____

_____

_____

_____

_____

_____

_____

_____

_____

_____

_____

_____

_____

_____

_____

_____

"If you abide in Me, and My words abide in you, you will ask
what you desire, and it shall be done for you."
John 15:7

Lead me in Your truth and teach me, for You are the God
of my salvation; for You I wait all the day long.
Psalm 25:5

"Give, and you will receive. Your gift will return to you in full—pressed down, shaken together to make room for more, running over."
Luke 6:38

_____

He will keep you strong to the end so that you will be free
from all blame on the day when our Lord Jesus Christ returns.
1 Corinthians 1:8

The reward for trusting Him will be the salvation of your souls.
1 Peter 1:9

_____

He who earnestly seeks good finds favor.
Proverbs 11:27

_____

_____

_____

_____

_____

_____

_____

_____

_____

_____

_____

_____

_____

_____

_____

_____

_____

_____

_____

_____

_____

_____

My soul clings to You; Your right hand upholds me.
Psalm 63:8

_____

May the God of hope fill you with all joy and peace as you trust in Him,
so that you may overflow with hope by the power of the Holy Spirit.
Romans 15:13

Keep me as the apple of Your eye; hide me in the shadow of Your wings.
Psalm 17:8

_____

_____

_____

_____

_____

_____

_____

_____

_____

_____

_____

_____

_____

_____

_____

_____

_____

_____

_____

_____

_____

_____

Because of the LORD's great love we are not consumed,
for His compassions never fail.
Lamentations 3:22

Praise God in His sanctuary; praise Him in His mighty heavens. Praise Him
for His acts of power; praise Him for His surpassing greatness.
Psalm 150:1-2

_____

_____

_____

_____

_____

_____

_____

_____

_____

_____

_____

_____

_____

_____

_____

_____

_____

_____

_____

_____

_____

_____

_____

_____

"I know the plans I have for you," declares the Lord, "plans to prosper you and not to harm you, plans to give you hope and a future."
Jeremiah 29:11

I will bless You as long as I live; in Your name I will lift up my hands.
Psalm 63:4

_____

_____

_____

_____

_____

_____

_____

_____

_____

_____

_____

_____

_____

_____

_____

_____

_____

_____

_____

_____

_____

"Come to Me, all of you who are weary and carry
heavy burdens, and I will give you rest."
Matthew 11:28

May the Lord of peace Himself give you peace at all times and in every way.
2 Thessalonians 3:16

Create in me a clean heart, O God, and renew a steadfast spirit within me.
Psalm 51:10

Sing for joy, O heavens, and exult, O earth; break forth,
O mountains, into singing! For the LORD has comforted His people.

Isaiah 49:13

_____

"Anything is possible if a person believes."
Mark 9:23

_____

_____

_____

_____

_____

_____

_____

_____

_____

_____

_____

_____

_____

_____

_____

_____

_____

_____

_____

_____

_____

_____

_____

"Peace I leave with you; My peace I give to you...
Let not your hearts be troubled, neither let them be afraid."
John 14:27

_____

Give thanks to the God of gods ... Give thanks to the Lord of lords ...
Give thanks to the God of heaven, for His steadfast love endures forever.
Psalm 136:2-3, 26

_____

_____
_____
_____
_____
_____
_____
_____
_____
_____
_____
_____
_____
_____
_____
_____
_____
_____
_____
_____
_____
_____
_____
_____

"No eye has seen, no ear has heard, and no mind has imagined
what God has prepared for those who love Him."
1 Corinthians 2:9

_____

Let us hold unswervingly to the hope we profess,
for He who promised is faithful.
Hebrews 10:23

_____

_____

_____

_____

_____

_____

_____

_____

_____

_____

_____

_____

_____

_____

_____

_____

_____

_____

_____

_____

_____

_____

Draw near to God, and He will draw near to you.
James 4:8

_____

Praise the name of the LORD, for His name alone is exalted;
His majesty is above earth and heaven.
Psalm 148:13

"I am with you always, even to the end of the age."
Matthew 28:20

_____

The Lord is good to all; He has compassion on all He has made.
Psalm 145:9

He who has begun a good work in you will complete it
until the day of Jesus Christ.
Philippians 1:6

_____

"Whoever comes to Me I will never cast out… For this is the will of My Father, that everyone who looks on the Son and believes in Him should have eternal life."

John 6:37, 40

_____

_____

_____

_____

_____

_____

_____

_____

_____

_____

_____

_____

_____

_____

_____

_____

_____

_____

_____

_____

_____

_____

Thank You for making me so wonderfully complex!
Your workmanship is marvelous—how well I know it.

Psalm 139:14

_____

If anything is excellent or praiseworthy—think about such things.
Philippians 4:8

Trust in the LORD forever,
for the LORD, the LORD Himself, is the Rock eternal.
Isaiah 26:4

_____

"You are the LORD, You alone. You have made heaven, the heaven of heavens ...
the earth and all that is on it ... and You preserve all of them."

Nehemiah 9:6

_____

_____

_____

_____

_____

_____

_____

_____

_____

_____

_____

_____

_____

_____

_____

_____

_____

_____

_____

_____

_____

_____

_____

We know that God causes everything to work together for the good of those
who love God and are called according to His purpose for them.
Romans 8:28

_____

God has said, "Never will I leave you; never will I forsake you."
So we say with confidence, "The Lord is my helper; I will not be afraid."
Hebrews 13:5-6

_____

_____

_____

_____

_____

_____

_____

_____

_____

_____

_____

_____

_____

_____

_____

_____

_____

_____

_____

_____

_____

_____

Happy are those who hear the joyful call to worship, for they will walk in
the light of Your presence, LORD.... They exult in Your righteousness.

Psalm 89:15-16

God is able to make all grace abound to you, so that having all sufficiency
in all things at all times, you may abound in every good work.
2 Corinthians 9:8

Sing a new song to the LORD! Sing His praises from the ends of the earth!

Isaiah 42:10

The Lord is good, a refuge in times of trouble. He cares for those who trust in Him.
Nahum 1:7

_____

_____

_____

_____

_____

_____

_____

_____

_____

_____

_____

_____

_____

_____

_____

_____

_____

_____

_____

_____

_____

_____

Cast all your anxiety on Him because He cares for you.
1 Peter 5:7

_____

"Blessing and glory and wisdom and thanksgiving and honor and power and might be to our God forever and ever! Amen."
Revelation 7:12

"May the LORD bless you and protect you. May the LORD smile on you and be gracious to you. May the LORD show you His favor and give you His peace."
Numbers 6:24-26

"The Lord your God is with you, He is mighty to save. He will take great delight in you, He will quiet you with His love, He will rejoice over you with singing."

Zephaniah 3:17

I will instruct you and teach you in the way you should go;
I will guide you with My eye.

Psalm 32:8

_____

For You are my rock and my fortress; and for Your
name's sake You lead me and guide me.
Psalm 31:3

_____

_____

_____

_____

_____

_____

_____

_____

_____

_____

_____

_____

_____

_____

_____

_____

_____

_____

_____

_____

_____

_____

_____

Search me, O God, and know my heart; test me and know my anxious thoughts.
Psalm 139:23

"I am the living bread that came down from heaven.
If anyone eats of this bread, he will live forever."
John 6:51

Those who wait on the Lord shall renew their strength;
they shall mount up with wings like eagles.
Isaiah 40:31

_____

_____

_____

_____

_____

_____

_____

_____

_____

_____

_____

_____

_____

_____

_____

_____

_____

_____

_____

_____

_____

_____

_____

O Lord, I will honor and praise Your name, for You are my God.
You do such wonderful things!

Isaiah 25:1

_____

With You is the fountain of life; in Your light do we see light.
Psalm 36:9

For as members of one body you are called to live in peace.
And always be thankful.
Colossians 3:15

_____

Pour out your hearts to Him, for God is our refuge.
Psalm 62:8

Be kind to one another, tenderhearted, forgiving one another,
even as God in Christ forgave you.
Ephesians 4:32

_____

Let not steadfast love and faithfulness forsake you ... write them on the tablet of
your heart. So you will find favor and good success in the sight of God and man.
Proverbs 3:3-4

Day by day the Lord takes care of the innocent,
and they will receive an inheritance that lasts forever.
Psalm 37:18

_____

Strive for full restoration, encourage one another, be of one mind,
live in peace. And the God of love and peace will be with you.
2 Corinthians 13:11

_____

_____

_____

_____

_____

_____

_____

_____

_____

_____

_____

_____

_____

_____

_____

_____

_____

_____

_____

_____

_____

_____

_____

_____

_____

Godliness with contentment is great gain.
1 Timothy 6:6

_____

May He give you the desire of your heart and
make all your plans succeed.
Psalm 20:4

_____

_____
_____
_____
_____
_____
_____
_____
_____
_____
_____
_____
_____
_____
_____
_____
_____
_____
_____
_____
_____
_____
_____

Every good gift and every perfect gift is from above.
James 1:17

May the God of peace ... equip you with everything good for doing His will ...
through Jesus Christ, to whom be glory for ever and ever.
Hebrews 13:20-21

How precious to me are Your thoughts, O God! How vast is the sum of them!
Psalm 139:17

As the deer longs for streams of water, so I long for You,
O God. I thirst for God, the living God.
Psalm 42:1-2

"I will not forget you! See, I have engraved you on the palms of My hands."
Isaiah 49:15-16

_____

Know that the LORD, He is God! It is He who made us, and we
are His; we are His people, and the sheep of His pasture.
Psalm 100:3

_____

"If you abide in Me, and My words abide in you, you will ask
what you desire, and it shall be done for you."
John 15:7

_____

Lead me in Your truth and teach me, for You are the God
of my salvation; for You I wait all the day long.
Psalm 25:5

_____

_____

_____

_____

_____

_____

_____

_____

_____

_____

_____

_____

_____

_____

_____

_____

_____

_____

_____

_____

_____

_____

"Give, and you will receive. Your gift will return to you in full—pressed
down, shaken together to make room for more, running over."

Luke 6:38

He will keep you strong to the end so that you will be free
from all blame on the day when our Lord Jesus Christ returns.
1 Corinthians 1:8

The reward for trusting Him will be the salvation of your souls.
1 Peter 1:9

He who earnestly seeks good finds favor.
Proverbs 11:27

My soul clings to You; Your right hand upholds me.
Psalm 63:8

_____

May the God of hope fill you with all joy and peace as you trust in Him,
so that you may overflow with hope by the power of the Holy Spirit.
Romans 15:13